I0720386

THE NEXT VERSE POETS MIXTAPE
VOLUME ONE: THE 4 X 4

Other titles from Central Square Press

A HARD SUMMATION by Afaa Michael Weaver
CRACKED CALABASH by Lisa Pegram

THE NEXT VERSE POETS MIXTAPE
VOLUME ONE: THE 4 X 4

poems

Melanie Henderson, Fred Joiner, Lisa Pegram, Enzo Silon Surin

CENTRAL SQUARE PRESS

Copyright © 2016 Central Square Press

All rights reserved. No part of this book may be used or reproduced in any manner whatsoever without written permission from the publisher, except in the case of brief quotations embodied in critical articles or reviews.

All inquiries and permissions requests should be addressed to the Publisher:

Central Square Press
publisher@centralsquarepress.com
www.centralsquarepress.com

Published in the United States of America
First Edition

ISBN-13: 978-1-941604-02-1

ISBN-10: 1941604021

Many thanks to the following publications in which these poems first appeared:

The 5X5 Project: "Seven Ways of Looking at Black Flowers"; The Academy of American Poets (poets.org) : "After Dinner"; The BreakBeat Poets: New American Poetry in the Age of Hip Hop: "Corners"; Iris G. Press' The Fledgling Rag: "Orchestra" and "Nostalgia" as part of the series poem, "B.O.N.E.S"; The Naugatuck River Review: "Sunday Autumn Afternoons in Jamaica, Queens"; sx salon: "The Ethereal Hour Elegy (Port-Au-Prince)"; Valley Voices: "Notes to a Little Black Boy";

Cover Design: Enzo Silon Surin

Cover Art is based on the photograph "If You Don't Use It" by Melanie Henderson

for the first verse

CONTENTS

INTRODUCTION

Melanie Henderson, Fred Joiner, Lisa Pegram, Enzo Silon Surin **THE NEXT VERSE POETS MIXTAPE VOLUME ONE: THE 4 X 4** poems Melanie Henderson, Fred Joiner, Lisa Pegram, Enzo Silon Surin **THE NEXT VERSE POETS MIXTAPE VOLUME ONE: THE 4 X 4** poems Melanie Henderson, Fred Joiner, Lisa Pegram, Enzo Silon Surin **THE NEXT VERSE POETS MIXTAPE VOLUME ONE: THE 4 X 4** poems Melanie Henderson, Fred Joiner, Lisa Pegram, Enzo Silon Surin **THE NEXT VERSE POETS MIXTAPE VOLUME ONE: THE 4 X 4** poems Melanie Henderson, Fred Joiner, Lisa Pegram, Enzo Silon Surin **THE NEXT VERSE POETS MIXTAPE VOLUME ONE: THE 4 X 4** poems Melanie Henderson, Fred Joiner, Lisa Pegram, Enzo Silon Surin **THE NEXT VERSE POETS MIXTAPE VOLUME ONE: THE 4 X 4** poems Melanie Henderson, Fred Joiner, Lisa Pegram, Enzo Silon Surin **THE NEXT VERSE POETS MIXTAPE VOLUME ONE: THE 4 X 4** poems Melanie Henderson, Fred Joiner, Lisa Pegram, Enzo Silon Surin **THE NEXT VERSE POETS MIXTAPE VOLUME ONE: THE 4 X 4** poems Melanie Henderson, Fred Joiner, Lisa Pegram, Enzo Silon Surin **THE NEXT VERSE POETS MIXTAPE VOLUME ONE: THE 4 X 4** poems Melanie Henderson, Fred Joiner, Lisa Pegram, Enzo Silon Surin **THE NEXT VERSE POETS MIXTAPE**

melanie henderson

NOTES TO A LITTLE BLACK BOY

1

There are no promises to your tribe.

2

Tribes of Amadou and Barack,
pastures run bloody green,
presidential red carpets, smiles,
hands that wave to proud citizens,
to embrace wife and daughters,
or hands risen to block an onslaught
of bullets, the blinding glare let off like
lightning from a tribe of hateful eyes,
a pack run amuck with thirst.

3

Little Boy, I am lying a bit; there is
some softness, some dreams bunched
on top a dandelion seed head. Just one,
promise. One blow. Hope. Guard. Wish.

4

At your birth, some woman tucked
away sweet bread in a cream colored
swaddle cloth; the wine is kept to mature
with you in a covered chalice for the day
you are ripe. For your tribe, this is cause
for ceremony, celebration.

5

Your hair, once moist, smooth, flat
on your scalp, tightens, dries, rises.
Arc of lion's back. Cultural memory,
a woman guarded the crater in your
skull from impact, poaching.

6

Still, Little Boy, I make you and yours
no promises. These eyes will keep watch
in your golden mud outskirts. We will
sit our big bottoms in the heirloom
rocking chair, seemingly preoccupied
with craft, string and needles, acknowledging
the lamp's gradation of dims, and the stranger
approaching, disheveling dust on the road.

BORN HOME

To begin at the beginning
& we are not from this place
We know   the snow
          doesn't fall in January,
the gum of July doesn't stick to the blood in our skin

& we are not from this place
We know   the rows of dependent houses
liberated by separating hues of a president,
my alarm clock's muteness, temporary
it's arteries, a blazing blue; it's 7:59

& we are not from this place
We know   how to begin at the beginning
when a high school is just a high school
& our rhythm is not smart
and we are not from this place

We know   the vacant eyes of our streets,
pots in the pavement sing
from this place we are from—

We know.

ORCHESTRA

Lay me at the fall line—

I will be more everlasting
than boat, vessel or memory.

You will know my music
when you go to forget me,

my buried bone will rumble
baritone at the shovel's kick,

my band, the river's flow
against uphill rock.

NOSTALGIA

It's not any different
than Southwest Washington,
or any other old black hood.

Georgetown is marble and
brick over blood and bone.
The tragedy is not its newness

—or even its color. It's a failure
of courtesy not to speak to us:
ghosts on lampposts, right brown

shoes sturdy on left knees,
elbows propping up hatted heads
from the chin; it's a failure

to remember we built those old
rock churches, and monuments,
those houses crumbled to erect

condos that block out light.
Take off your hat when entering
this city; there are spirits around you.

fred joiner

CURRENCY

a pocket can sometimes be
a kind of prison.
I have never lived in
a cash economy where the bill
fold unfolds to find someone
creased in the middle,
but perhaps credit moves
the same, the way it scores
the pocket and the body
boxed & bureaued-
the edge of a card
cuts anything akin to skin
a Dollar, a Euro, a World
Bank, a debt to erase,
a race, a weight.

SEVEN WAYS OF LOOKING AT BLACK FLOWERS

> *XIII*
> *What is more beautiful than black flowers,*
> *Or the Blackmen in fields*
> *Gathering them?*
> *– Raymond Patterson, Twenty-Six Ways of Looking at a Blackman*

I

In what mellow tone
Do black flowers
Sing their blues?

II

Black flowers like black
Hands – colored: reaching toward
A mystery. Up South.

III

Black flowers, the gift
Of open palms
Facing North, but
Rooted South

IV

A man and a woman
Are one
A man and a woman and black flowers
Are dust

V

Against a sky white
Like a fists full of Sea
Island cotton the sky raining
Blood on black flowers

VI

In our world/ The tongue speaks
Only a binary song, always a black
Flowering problem, against a white
Canvas —blood in between

VII

The sound possibilities of black flowers
Were choices made by the hands, breath
And brass of a gifted man
Looking inward, blood on his lips

DRUM LESSON

for Naomi Skye

I have heard
            Komunyakaa's Kadoom,
the thrum of Hippie digits
                on taut alien skin;
sat in caccophonus drum circles,
                a circus;
the body of my generation is
                filled with Boom
Bap and breaking,
                Premier's crisp snaps,
Dilla's twisted tympani's
                Pete Rock pan mix
all our attempts to keep
                our um boom
baboom booming – Baraka sound science.
                I am still rocked by the blood
of Blakey's hard swing mosaic,
the insisting Roach,
the sound of Elvin's engine.

But today, in the slow swing

of a rocking chair,
first girl, swaddled in my arms
I learn that the body
is drum & the hand follows
                the heart;
all the drumming
I need.

SONS OF

hidden stylus' frantic scratch,
sound took tenements' lack
& made art, made movement –
the physics of the rocked body,
the philosophy of the body politic,

& a need to be heard,
another sonic cry birthed
by necessity, that speaks
to the least of these

spontaneous opus composed
at moment's notice, spun, turn
tables backspinning vinyl mid
night on the right
hand & to the break
of dawn, spun forward,
on the left like a cosmic
time machine.

we are the new herdsman of synergy,
our heads nod by choice, affirmation
our bodies respond to the call
of another, oom boom ba boom

bap born in blood
like a thunderclap in the swelter
of summer night

& in the break,
we take
the needle
that broke
the dance
& make
a new song,
a new thing.

lisa pegram

LAMB & VODKA

In my favorite photo of my aunt,
she's sitting on a picnic blanket in Iceland
in her bra and a pencil skirt.

This is not tourist behavior. She lives there.

Whenever it hit anything close to 70 degrees, we stopped
whatever we were doing, took off our clothes
and went outside.

Her hair, which I have always known as a colossal afro,
is straight. A globe of fat satin curls, clearly the result
of a perfect set on big plastic rollers under a hooded dryer.

Where does a black girl from Virginia get her hair done in
1960s Reykjavik?

She is young and laughing
with the husband I never met. An impromptu feast of lamb,
vodka, sweet mustard and dried onions at their feet.

He points at something I can't see in the distance.

The photo is black and white, except the defiant blue
of his eyes which reflect the sky more than having a color
of their own. They are the shade of fjords,

nested between rugged cliffs of jaw and brow.

This husband I never knew, echoed in my cousins
who call our grandparents Amma and Afi
their love of family, vast as glaciers.
The Reyka and tonic we sip at cocktail hour.
The salmon we swapped for turkey one Thanksgiving.

I wonder who took this photo.

Mossy plateau yawns around them for miles,
but there are no trees. Roots are no match
for volcanic ash. There is a bubbling lagoon.
Air so clean it sparkles. Cathedrals of ice
in the background. And a fire, molten,
throbbing beneath the surface.

MOONSHINE, 1931

Millie found him.

Charlie Smith, bootlegger from North Carolina,
learned quick that country and Caribbean favor
each other, first cousins born of twin sisters.

Bare feetPig's feetDusty roadsHot. Fast money,
wardrobes built of primary colors and grudges
held longer than a redbone's braid
paroled from the bun at her nape. Stronger

than dark liquor noosing throats come Friday night.
Hiss, drawl or brogue:

> *I'll cut ya.*

Moonshine cast its glow over sweet Millie
who wound her waist in the spotlight.
This new country, where her brothers could count—
but she could count and read—made her Queen Bee.

Millie brought Charlie.

Charlie brought the honey. Sticky
hexagonal cells in a Harlem brownstone.
Top floor: The Bathtub
Middle floor: The Still

Bottom Floor: The Bottles
Basement: The Bank.

Big black business leads to big black Buick
Leads to big black britches. Millie say "partner"
Charlie say "franchise." But

                        who a worker bee without The Queen?

Charlie say: *Stay in yo place, woman.*

Charlie say: *Harlem be ours, Staten be mine.*

Charlie say: *Whatchu know about a Southern boy's fury?*

Millie say:

I from so far sout, Cackalacky look like Boston.
What the ras ya know about the equator?

Revenge is a bell with a mace for a clapper,
every boast a steep climb up Mount Gay. Charlie,
from farmers. Millie from pirates. Walk the plank.

I'll cut ya.
Charlie never could keep that big black car in his lane.
Kids would stop streetball—mid play—at the sight of him.
Run screaming for the sidewalk.

Wasn't til the babiest nephew, the streetball captain, had

grown a bald spot
and forked roads at the corners of his eyes
that Millie confessed over Dewar's neat:

She made the call.

Brought the raid on the hive,
tropical storm on Charlie's head,
one night working late. Alone
in the brownstone. Lusty siren

screaming red. Handcuffs. Gavel.
20 years wondering who

made the call?

His first call when he got out: *Millie...*
She gave him a basement apartment.
A job as super in one of the many properties
she had acquired. He shoveled her snow.
Unclogged her toilets. Cleaned her gutters
til the day he died. He never
knew. Millie made the call.

A vexed Bajan can beat the devil at a grudge.

> *He was on his ass when I met him and that's where I left*
> *him.*

AFTER DINNER

What is said in conversation
when all of the women leave
the room? Satin glove slipped
from fist. An uncut deck of cards.

The men show their teeth. Mark
opinions like territory. Laugh
upside down, wrinkles shape-
shifting between stone, wood

and flesh. This cut & paste debate
sits in the shade of cigar smoke.
Sips dark liquors neat, no chaser.
Spans home front and auction block.

Laughter and shit talk roll
like distant thunder. Make bridges
of fragments. End in guarded
embraces as quick as they are firm.

THE ROMAN BATHS

I.
Thermae, Latin.
Public baths visited daily, several
hours of soak, sweat and socialization.

All Romans of all classes welcome,
except slaves
stoking the furnaces below.

II.
Metro station, Newborn morning.
Above ground is still. Snoring. Beneath,
trains shovel sepia workers
toward smoldering jobs they did not steal,
but overpaid for. Tool belts, hard hats
and feather dusters transform ideas
into monuments. Then keep them clean.

III.
Apodyterium: Pay a fee, strip.
Have a slave anoint you with oil,
and tuck your clothes away.
Keep your sandals to spare your soiled feet—

don't let the heat close enough to touch you.

IV.
Rush hour legions pound snooze
before rising for coffee and fruit
picked by loved ones or countrymen
these dawn faces left behind.

The workers clutch thermoses and lunch

bags that sweat evidence of their contents.

V.
Hypocaust: The Furnace.

Fornacatores: Its keepers.

Man made hot springs.

VI.
Masters of the city dream in blue print,
while the vertebrae align at the turnstile
to strike the match that ignites white
marble floor.

The water simmers.

VII.
Many public baths adjoined the forum.

VIII.
Washington, DC is haunted by ancient Rome.
Alabaster columns built on swampland,
sinking one blink at a time.

IX.
Ruins—
A bath without water
is just crumbling walls.

X.
It's a wonder those slaves
didn't gorge those fires. Lock windows. Doors.
Stew naked captors 'til meat fell tender off of bone,
like Abuelita's famous sancocho.

enzo silon surin

CORNERS

Outside Papi's Bodega, young boy in
summer's native garb—white tank-top,

doorag's a smooth blue crown garnishing
the stubbles of a week-old fade—regulates

a stereo knob while sitting shotgun
in a chromed-wheel Escalade—the ghost

of Tupac Shakur magnified in a sub-
woofer like an opus—as long as

music's kept all's good where we come
from. If only a glare didn't easily stumble—

if only manhood wasn't tenured with black
powder in metal capsules, brown boys, free

to chase arcade mortality, wouldn't have to
warily long for a ghetto's heaven or if grief,

inherited each day they step into the a.m.,
would follow them into an afterlife.

But corners often leave souls open and closed,

hopin' for more...and on Winthrop and Thorndale

the sidewalk folds into a man in hooded sweat-
shirt and blood-sodden jeans, fresh breaths

breaching his lungs—if only keeping eyes off
the karma and on the prize was what made this

world go 'round, it would be what was always
wanted—any landscape better than what's here

—where on most nights, a native glare renders
a chamber empty as winter flower boxes.

ONCE, WHEN WE WERE NOT GODS

Don't paint yourself into a corner, they'd say,
which would imply we had a choice; would
imply we had a say in the selection: the brush,
the paint, and the room—corners to edge
bodies with sharp elbows and knees into.

A room with corners is not a room, isn't
a city is not a choice. What we were taught,
it was wrong. A choice is not a choice if one
didn't have a say in the options—if we had
a choice in the making of options we would
be gods. But no matter—ardent vow or ache
for calling each other God—we were not.

The corner is where we grappled with full
knowledge we were naked. And today I am
a ball in the corner of my bathroom recalling
playmates who made a corner their epistle
as a result of the interior made inferior.
We were taught that all corners were bad
places where idle things go to collect dust.

Yet New York City was filled with many
such rooms, to be trapped in. Could it be
our demise was planned? And the choices

we made were not choices but decisions,
and the selections we made a consequence
of not being gods and not the ones to father
options? To paint oneself in a corner means
one has a say: in the brush and the paint, and
in canvasing rooms with deliberate corners.

HOW TO NULLIFY A SUPER HERO

At the edge of a bed's stoop—
pillowcase cape, plunger
as dagger—avenger of wrongs
interrogating a whimsical city

filled with sirens and choppers,
cops dwelling in dark alleys—
stymied in ambush of ski-masked
robbers. Imagined your superhero

telephone ringing, a frantic voice—
Shawn, who lived down the hall,
—in need of help to bolster late-
night raids. Dreamt of being a cop,

the raiment of NYPD blue—wanting
to bring solace to a uniformed hue
Haitian families akin to the Tonton
Macoutes. That would change.

Calling out to phantom crooks—
lay down your weapons—your best
Lion-O from the ThunderCats—
awing at a sky urged into clamor

with your plunger—playing the part
'til the wind that framed your chocolate
milk-mustached face, tucked you
in bed—a decade long slumber.

*

When you woke, Shawn no longer
wanted to be a cop and your dagger-
breaking news: Abner Louima—
arrested outside a Brooklyn nightclub—

hand-held radio and fist-battered—
later at a precinct, plunger's handle
—rapine. Later still, interrogation:
his brown body sluggish as yours,

eyes swollen in that eclipsed room.
Started fearing that you entered
the wrong skin at birth—into a
blunt country, a barrow world—

musing on Batman and Robin—what
did they do on their off-days—when
out of frame, with their utility belts,
in Gotham's whisted and dark alleys?

THE ETHEREAL HOUR ELEGY

Port-au-Prince

There are times when the night is bad
but the sleep good, when in the womb-
shack of the city, dormant as a seed,
we nestle in a succulent dream—

the wet carcass of a blue tarp as second
skin—when tears are notably reliable
and drain the body of a toxin once kin—
these are nights when the night is good

but the sleep bad—when we wonder
if I cried who would hear me but the moon?
—allayed with the question: good nights
and bad dreams or the antipode? I answer

the body's an experience; I answer take a look—
those mountains, less than a mile from here,
slopes rising up in the meanest air as though
they were building a way out of no way—

does it help to know this is how we spend
our time, a strange math on our tongues?
Conceiting often gets an upper hand. I answer
how much longer will you search for meaning

in clouds, neglecting the moon? Can no longer
say what it is like here—many times we have
assigned words, set out in your direction,
and we never hear whether they arrive or not.

bonus

tracks

THE BAJAN FLAG

I flew my first at Carnival. Boston.
Tucked into the back winding
        waistband of skin-tight
           sky blue
        capri pants—a bridal train.

Yellow halter top, whistle between my teeth. My locks,
Rapunzel then, flirted with the flag. Black pendulum

        advancing.   Receding.

Dipping roti skin in curry gravy, sipping
sorrell shandy, everything first time

        yet familiar.   *My first trip home:*

Twenty-three years old at full gallop. No
reins. On the bus from the airport,

        I caught the hem of the sea

in scratchy window flashes between hotel & store fronts.
At full stop I bolted. Sandals & possessions abandoned to
sand.

Walked waist deep into surf, my linen skirt—

a white flag billowing. Pledging.

SOVEREIGNTY

Can be fragile, easy
to fade or be erased, all
It takes is a single heavy hand,
a legend thrown
Like a gauntlet, the hand that opens
an island's body, an autopsy.
Nothing says empire
like a flag, says republic like fabric
Stretched & strung, swathes
of land tethered, a sanguine stitch
Of the tongue, language conquers
from within   before the blade
Separates flesh & kin,
breath & the line, all
Broken by a wall
& a people's history
Crumbling in another's wake

JOY

sifts for black
in the blush of a summer lily,

the fat style in my upper chest,
breath given to sun,
out of light, lung plucking,
windless, spiraling,
a cork breaking cylinders
for berries, wine

if you knew, anther,
how strong the absence
of your skin,

touches, unsettles
pollen, sprinkled flour
in this yard, seeking to
properly break color,
mush petal & peduncle
into dye.

ON SUNDAY AUTUMN AFTERNOONS IN JAMAICA, QUEENS

we trusted
our bodies cutting into
the fat bold air

in hand-me-down
layers—pigskin
against our ribs

like a Hughes' weighted dream—
no pads, no helmets for the journey
of grabs and leaps. We toiled

until the field faded—and
alone and out of breath,
we talked and laughed, waded—

the accumulation of out-and-gone days
—some of the things we'd never said
said, as if this would carry into real life.

about the next verse poets

MELANIE HENDERSON, Washington, DC native poet, editor, photographer and publisher, is the author of Elegies for New York Avenue, winner of the 2011 Main Street Rag Poetry Book Award. An alumnus of Howard and Trinity Universities, she studied poetry at Howard University in Dr. Tony Medina's "Boot Camp" and at the Voices Summer Writing Workshops (VONA) in San Francisco, CA prior to earning an MFA from Lesley University in Cambridge, MA. Her poems have appeared in Beltway Poetry Quarterly, Drumvoices Revue, jubilat, Torch, Tuesday; An Art Project, Valley Voices, and The Washington Informer among others. She is a recipient of the 2009 Larry Neal Writers Award and received a 2013 Pushcart Prize nomination from Iris G. Press. She is a Founding Editor of Tidal Basin Review.

FRED JOINER is a poet and curator living in Bamako, Mali. His work has appeared Callaloo, Gargoyle, and Fledgling Rag, PLUCK! among other publications. Joiner is a two-time winner of the Larry Neal Award for Poetry and a 2014 Artist Fellowship Winner as awarded by the D.C. Commission on the Arts and Humanities. As a curator of art or public programming, Joiner has worked with the American Poetry Museum, Belfast Exposed Gallery (Northern Ireland), Hillyer Artspace, Honfleur Gallery, Medina Galerie (Bamako, Mali), the Phillips Collection, the Prince Georges African American Museum and Cultural Center, the Reginald F. Lewis Museum, Smithsonian's National Museum of African Art's and more. He is the co-founder of The Center for Poetic Thought at the Monroe Street Market in the Brookland neighborhood of Washington, D.C.

LISA PEGRAM is a DC native poet, essayist and author of the chapbook, Cracked Calabash (Central Square Press, 2015.) Her work has been published by Random House, Black Classic Press, Poets.org, The Independent film magazine, and L'Officiel, India, among others. She has over 15 years of experience facilitating high-level arts programming for organizations such as the Smithsonian Institute and National Geographic. Her poetry has been set to classical music and performed at Georgetown University, Haverford College, Columbia University and St. Matthew's Cathedral. Awards include: DC Mayor's Arts Award "Outstanding Emerging Artist", Larry Neal Writer's Award Finalist and International Women's Conference Co-Chair. She completed her MFA in 2012 and is currently based in Curacao where she is a writing professor and a personal chef.

ENZO SILON SURIN is a Haitian-born poet, publisher, advocate and author of the chapbook Higher Ground (Finishing Line Press, 2006). He is a Pushcart nominee and the 2015 PEN New England Celebrated New Voice in Poetry. His poems have appeared in Jubilat, Soundings East, The BreakBeat Poets: New American Poetry in the Age of Hip-Hop, Naugatuck River Review, sx salon, Tidal Basin Review, and The Caribbean Writer, among others. His manuscript, *When My Body Was A Clinched Fist,* was selected as a semi-finalist for the 2015 Philip Levine Poetry Book Prize. Surin holds an MFA in Creative Writing from Lesley University and is Associate Professor of English at Bunker Hill Community College. He is also founder and publisher at Central Square Press.

NOTES:

1. "Corners" contains the lyric "leave souls open and closed, hopin' for more" from the rap song "The Corner" by Hip Hop artist Common.

2. "Seven Ways of Looking at Black Flowers" is inspired by the Gene Davis's painting *Black Flowers,* Raymond Patterson's poem, "Twenty-Six Ways of Looking at a Blackman", and Wallace Stevens's poem, "Thirteen Ways of looking at a Blackbird".

www.ingramcontent.com/pod-product-compliance
Lightning Source LLC
Chambersburg PA
CBHW071842190726
48292CB00005B/1872